Published by
Gallery Books
An imprint of W H Smith Publishers Inc.
112 Madison Avenue
New York, New York 10016 USA

Produced by
Twin Books
15 Sherwood Place
Greenwich, CT 06830 USA

ISBN 0-8317-2304-1

Printed in Hong Kong

Fun with Words
On Vacation

Twin Books

GALLERY BOOKS
An imprint of W.H. Smith Publishers Inc.
112 Madison Avenue
New York, New York 10016

AT THE BEACH

Baby Mickey has found a big  , and he is

listening for the sound of the ocean. Baby Minnie

is sitting under an  because the sun is so

hot. She looks surprised because a little

has caught hold of her skirt and won't let go. Baby

Donald has just finished building a big  ,

and Baby Pete is trying to crawl through the gate.

Watch out, Baby Pete ! Baby Donald doesn't want

you to knock down his castle. Isn't Baby Minnie's

 pretty ? The Disney Babies love

to spend a day at the beach.

Umbrella

Sand Castle

Crab

Seashell

Bath Towel

AT THE ZOO

Baby Horace has come to the zoo especially to see

the  in his pen. The giraffe is having just as

much fun looking at Baby Horace. Baby Donald and

Baby Daisy have made friends with the  .

Baby Goofy likes the soft striped coat of the

 . Nearby is another member of the

cat family : the  who is showing his teeth.

Baby Minnie is watching an animal that looks just

like her favorite stuffed toy, the black-and-white

 . Look ! Isn't that a

sitting on the fence of the kangaroo's cage ?

Giraffe

Lion

Tiger

Panda

Peacock

Kangaroo

ANIMALS IN THE ZOO

In a special part of the zoo are animals

one can pet and feed. The little

is ready to nibble the sugar cube in Baby

Mickey's hand. Baby Gus would like to touch

the little  who is just starting

to grow horns. Baby Gyro has had a surprise :

The 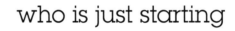 reached out and grabbed

his pants ! Baby Horace has had a wonderful

slow ride on the back of the 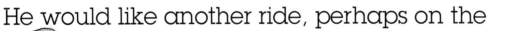 .

He would like another ride, perhaps on the

this time. Have you been to the zoo ?

Tortoise

Elephant

Monkey

Zebra

Antelope

AT THE CIRCUS

All the Disney Babies are getting into the act at the

circus ! The elephant is showing Baby Gyro how

well he can balance on his hind legs. Baby Minnie is

practicing to be a  . Baby Daisy

waits for her turn on the horse and holds a bag of

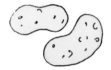 . Baby Goofy is all dressed up in a funny

hat and nose. He wants to be a  , and he's

playing a clown trick on Baby Pete. Baby Mickey

wants to be a  . He is juggling four bright

balls at once. What would you like to do if you

could join the circus ?

Peanuts

Bareback Rider

Clown

Juggler

AT THE AMUSEMENT PARK

The music of the  fills the air as

Baby Minnie and Baby Goofy go round and round.

Baby Minnie waves at Baby Mickey with her

 . Look ! Baby Goofy is sitting on his

horse backwards. He's saving his  to eat

when he gets off. Baby Donald is driving a

 , and so is Baby Pete. This is Baby

Pete's favorite ride. He loves bumping into Baby

Donald as hard as he can. Behind Baby Mickey and

Baby Daisy is the . Everyone wants to

ride on it because it is so high.

Ferris Wheel

Merry-go-round

Candy Apple

Hot-dog

Bumper
Car

AT THE AIRPORT

The Disney Babies think that the airport is one of

the most exciting things about taking a trip. Look at

the 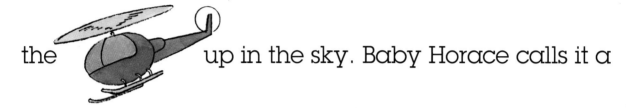 up in the sky. Baby Horace calls it a

whirlybird. Baby Pluto is pulling on a heavy

wheeled  while Baby Gyro rides. Baby

Clarabelle watches the  carry out the

boxes of luggage to be loaded aboard the waiting

 . Baby Mickey sees a tall tower in the

distance. It is the  . The people inside

tell the planes when and where they can land at the

busy airport. Everyone is going on vacation today !

Helicopter

Control Tower

Airplane

Baggage Cart

Suitcase

THE BIRTHDAY PARTY

The Disney Babies have been invited to a

birthday party. Brightly colored

fly through the air as Baby Mickey and Baby Minnie

play. They are making a lot of noise ! Baby Gyro's

 are in danger. Baby Goofy might pin the

tail on him, instead of the donkey ! There is a pretty

green ribbon wrapped around a big  .

It won't be opened until everyone has had some

 . Baby Donald has been keeping an

eye on the cake all day. He hopes someone will

blow out the  soon !

Streamers

Balloons

Candles

Present

Birthday Cake

WE GO SWIMMING

It is a very hot day, and the Disney Babies are

playing in the  . Baby Minnie and

Baby Mickey are playing catch with a beach ball.

Baby Mickey has a  that holds him up

in the water. Baby Daisy is wearing a new ,

which matches her suit. She is showing her friends

how well she can slide down the  . Be

careful, Baby Daisy. Don't fall on Baby Donald with

his tugboat and rubber duck. Now Baby Goofy

wants to use the water slide. He will climb up to it on

the little  .

Bathing Cap

Ladder

Water Slide

Rubber Float

Swimming Pool

WE GO CAMPING

It is twilight, and the Disney Babies are camping out.

Baby Clarabelle has spilled the  She must

pick it up. Baby Minnie is unpacking the food from

her  , and a little hedgehog has wandered

into the camp to see if there is a treat for him, too.

They have already put up the  to sleep in.

It has a screened window to keep the insects out.

But one little  has already found Baby Pete,

who has crawled into his  . Baby Pete

doesn't like camping out very much. He would

rather be home in his own bed.

Tent

Canteen

Backpack

Firefly

Sleeping Bag

IN THE DESERT

The Disney Babies are on a trip to the desert. The

sun is very hot there, but they find shade under the

 . Baby Donald has just discovered that the

rock he was sitting on is really a tortoise, which is a

kind of land turtle. Baby Pete has just stuck his

finger with a sharp  spine. And Baby Goofy is

worried. He thinks he is being chased by a friendly

 , who wants to play. It takes awhile to

feel at home in the desert, but the little  is

very happy there. He is sunning himself on a rock so

that he can stay warm through the cold desert night.

Coyote Pup

Palm Tree

Cactus

Lizard

It is a beautiful day to be out in a  , so the

Disney Babies have gone fishing. Baby Donald is

pushing the boat with a pole, and Baby Mickey is

throwing out the  . He hopes they will make a

good catch. Baby Minnie has followed them, but she

doesn't know how to use a  very well.

Uh-oh ! Baby Minnie has caught Baby Mickey's

pants with the . Baby Mickey is so surprised

that he drops the net, and his only catch gets away.

What a lucky  ! Next time, he'll stay away

from Babies in boats.

Fishing Pole

Boat

Hook

Net

Fish

OUR FAVORITE COLORS

The Disney Babies love bright colors. Baby Donald

is painting a flower with  leaves. He is

holding the tube of paint in one hand. Baby Minnie

is painting a vase a sunny  . She thinks it is

much prettier than the original color, which was

a darker tint of  . Baby Pluto just jumped on

Baby Pete and knocked over the  paint.

Luckily, he didn't trip on the pot of paint Donald used

to paint his flower, which is 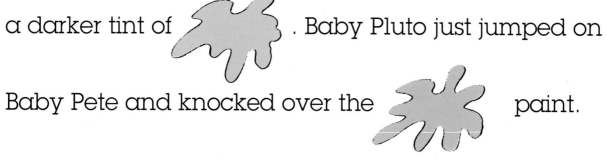 . The Disney

Babies have been rather messy with their paints.

Who will clean them up ?

Green

Lilac

Blue

Yellow

White

AT THE TRAIN STATION

Watch the train come down the  . Baby

Pete likes being the engineer and driving through

the dark and out again. Baby Donald wants

the train to stop for him. He is sitting on his suitcase.

Baby Pluto is enjoying his ride as he snoozes in the

 . Baby Mickey and Baby Minnie have

just passed the 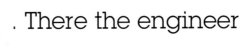 . There the engineer

gets water to make the steam that pushes the

 along the track. All aboard ! A train

ride is a fine way to see the countryside on

your vacation.

Water Tower

Tunnel

Track

Freight Car

Engine

WE LOOK AT BOATS

All the Disney Babies like to go to the water and

ride the boats. Everyone has a favorite. Baby

Mickey likes the strong little  that can pull

a string of heavy barges. But today the tugboat is

pulling Baby Mickey on a  and tooting its

whistle. Who is that speeding by and splashing

everyone ? It is Baby Pete in a 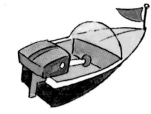 . He is

being very rude, and cutting right in front of Baby

Donald, who is paddling in a . Baby Daisy

likes flowers and shutters, and she can have both on

the .

Canoe

Motorboat

Houseboat

Raft

Tugboat

MORE FAVORITE COLORS

The Disney Babies are playing in Baby Donald's

back yard. Baby Donald is pushing Baby Daisy in

the ▮ wooden swing. Baby Goofy is waiting

his turn and looking at the pretty ▮ flower.

The butterfly flying over the flower has beautiful

▮ wings. Baby Goofy has ▮ pyjamas.

Baby Pete is pulling on Baby Pluto's leash, but Baby

Pluto doesn't want to go with Baby Pete. He pulls

back so hard that Baby Pete falls down and gets dirt

all over his ▮ shirt. He will need a clean

one when he gets home.

Brown

Grey

Green

Red

Orange

ON A PICNIC

The Disney Babies have spread a tablecloth on the

grass and opened their  . It is full of

good things to eat. Baby Pete takes a big bite of his

ham  , but Baby Donald won't eat

his bread until he has poured  all over it.

You can hardly see it under all that ketchup ! Baby

Daisy is handing a  to Baby Minnie, but

Baby Minnie doesn't want to take it because there is

an on it. Baby Mickey is laughing at her. He

doesn't know there are three ants on his .

Eating outdoors is fun.

Sandwich

Ketchup

Picnic Basket

Cookies

Ant

Paper Plate

OUR EARTH

Baby Mickey is using his color slides to tell his

friends about our Earth. The big body of water he's

pointing to is a . The lake was formed by

streams, springs, and the high that

splashes down into the lake. In the background is

a snow-capped . Between one mountain

and another is a low place called a  that

separates them. One of the mountains has a steep

rocky place where the soil has fallen away. This is

called a . Baby Donald and Baby Pete are

learning a lot !

A TRIP TO THE COUNTRY

The Disney Babies love to spend a summer day in

the country. Baby Pete is on the  throwing a

rock into the water with a big splash. He has startled a

 and gotten Baby Goofy all wet at the same

time. Poor Baby Goofy ! Baby Mickey is trying to

pick a for Baby Minnie, but it is hard work,

because the roots are so deep. He has disturbed a

brightly colored , which is flying off to

dry its wings somewhere else. Baby Minnie is happy

to crawl through the grass after a playful .

What do you like about the country ?

Bridge

Frog

Cattails

Dragonfly

Grasshopper

OUR SUMMER CONCERT

Strike up the band ! Baby Donald, the conductor,

keeps everyone in time with his baton. Baby Goofy is

tootling happily on his  in all the right places.

Baby Minnie is listening carefully so that she'll

know when to strum her  . Baby Pete doesn't

care about keeping time. He just wants to make a

very loud noise on his , so he plays right

through everyone else's part. Baby Daisy is doing a

good job on the , and Baby Mickey joins in

and blows hard on his .What a lovely noise

they are making !

AT THE AQUARIUM

Hardly anything is more fun than going to the

aquarium to look at all the sea creatures. Baby

Mickey thinks that the many-legged

is the most interesting animal. He is counting its

legs on his fingers. Baby Pete is teasing the

because it can't bite him. If it could,

he'd be pretty scared ! Two of the animals are so

smart that they can play ball. The   catches

the ball from Baby Gyro on his nose, while the

tries to get it away. Who is that little bird

who wants to play, too ? It's the   !

44

Shark

Octopus

Dolphin

Sea Lion

Penguin